Union Oyster House

COOKBOOK

Recipes and History from
America's Oldest Restaurant

Union Oyster House

COOKBOOK

Recipes and History from America's Oldest Restaurant

Jean Kerr and Spencer Smith

Seapoint Books
An imprint of Smith/Kerr Associates LLC
Kittery Point, Maine
www.SmithKerr.com

Distributed to the trade by National Book Network.
Generous quantity discounts are available from Smith/Kerr
Associates LLC (207) 703-2314 or www.SmithKerr.com.

Cataloging-in-Publication data is on file at the Library of
Congress.

ISBN-13: 978-0-9786899-1-9
ISBN-10: 0-9786899-1-7

Cover and book design by Claire MacMaster,
Barefoot Art Graphic Design
Printed in China through Printworks Int Ltd

Dedication

For all our patrons whom we have served
generation after generation

The Milano Family

Contents

PHOTO CREDITS:

Glenn Scott Photography pages 2, 9, 43, 46, 64, 69, 70, 78, 80, 87, 88, 91, 100, 103, 106, 109, 113, 117, 122, 127

National Park Service page 28

Conversion Table

Liquids

U.S. Measures	Metric (approximate)
1/2 TSP	2.5 ML
1 TSP	5 ML
1 TBS	15 ML
1/2 cup or 4 fluid oz.	120 ML
1 cup or 8 fluid oz. or 1/2 pint	240 ML
4 cups or 2 pints or 1 quart	950 ML
4 quarts or 1 gallon	3.8 L

Dry Ingredients

U.S. Measures	Metric (approximate)
1 oz.	30 g
8 oz or 1/2 lb.	230 g
16 oz or 1 lb	450 g

Acknowledgments

Chef Bill Coyne and past chefs
Management Team: Jim Malinn and Pattie Burke
Family: Jill Milano, Angelo Picardi, and Michael Milano Picardi
Ancillary Staff: Jean Hayes and Kathy Street
Historians: Arthur Krim and Ralph Eshelman
Artists: Doug Alvord and Stan Kotzen
Restaurant Review: James Ringrose
Photography: Ray Cavicchio and Michael Indresano
Editorial Consultant: Jane Manthorne

The authors would like to thank the Milano Family, and the staff of the Union Oyster House for the opportunity to work on this wonderful project. We are also grateful to our designer, Claire MacMaster, Glenn Scott for his superb photography, Kara Steere for her careful copyediting, Vicki Kasabian for her painstaking proofreading, and Kathleen Rocheleau for her indexing services. We would also like to thank Josh and Sasha Held for their support, as well as our trusty tasters and testers including Paula Sullivan, Diane Geise, and Ann and Bill Heafy and family.

Our thanks also to Senator Kennedy, Thomas O'Conner, Bobby Flay, and the Freedom Trail Foundation as well as the artists and photographers whose work graces these pages.

Foreword

Some of my fondest memories growing up in Boston are of my grandfather John Fitzgerald who loved to take my brothers and sisters and me on tours of the city he loved so much. We often visited the North End to see the Old North Church and other historic landmarks, but our final stop of the day was always the same—the Union Oyster House.

It's been a favorite of our family ever since. In Jack's campaign for the House in the 1940s and the Senate in the 1950s, we'd come back to the Oyster House after many a day on the campaign trail. Jack had his own favorite booth, No. 18, where he'd often read the newspaper, enjoy a delicious meal, and catch up with family and friends. I still go back as often as I can today.

I'm delighted that the Oyster House has decided to share its special recipes. This beautiful volume is an invitation to everyone, residents and visitors alike, to create and savor those famous dishes at home. They'll always be a little tastier, though, when they're served in the unique atmosphere of the Oyster House itself.

I'll never forget the many wonderful occasions when we dined at the restaurant and enjoyed its magnificent food and hospitality that always made it such a beloved part of life in Boston for many. May it remain so for generations to come.

Senator Edward M. "Ted" Kennedy

The Union Oyster House Today

The Union Oyster House Family

In 2003, the Union Oyster House in Boston, Massachusetts, was designated a National Historic Landmark and deservedly so. While America's oldest restaurant can now seat many more people than it did when it opened its doors in 1826, any one of the historic figures who frequented the place would recognize the classic semicircular oyster bar that is still the historic heart of the building. Statesman and orator Daniel Webster, who was an almost daily customer, would be right at home perched on a wooden stool at the soapstone bar ordering his usual tumblers of brandy and water, and six or more plates of oysters at a sitting.

Today, the Union Oyster House is owned and run by the Milano family. Joe Milano Sr. purchased the restaurant in 1970, and it is still very much a family business. Joe Milano Jr. and his sister Mary Ann Milano Picardi operate it. Their mother, Mary, now in her nineties, can be found overseeing the comings and goings from her desk by one of the front windows. The Milanos have been faithful stewards of this historic gem, as have the three previous owners. The wooden booths, formerly known as "stalls," that you see when you walk in the front door are original. The moment you enter, there is a feeling that you have stepped into a wonderful time capsule.

So what has changed over the years? The restaurant can now seat more than five hundred people in eight dining areas. More than half a million people a year visit the Union Oyster House to dine on oysters and other great New England dishes. Atwood & Bacon—as the Union Oyster House was called when it first opened—featured three kinds of oysters served stewed, roasted, fried, or raw. Accompaniments were simple dishes such as toast, dropped eggs, or crackers and milk with five kinds of pie available for dessert.

ATWOOD & BACON,

ESTABLISHED 1826.

OYSTERS.

VIRGINIA:

Stewed,	15
" large,	20
Roast,	15
" Fancy	20

NARRAGANSETT:

Raw, plate,	15
Half-Shell, doz.	15
" half-doz.	10
Stewed,	25
" bench-opened,	30
Roast,	25
" bench-opened,	30
Fried, crumbs or batter,	25
" bench-opened,	35
Roast in shell,	35

CAPES:

Half-shell, doz.	20
" half-doz.	10
Stewed,	35
Roast,	35
Fried,	40
Roast in shell,	40

CLAMS.

IPSWICH:

Stewed,	15
Steamed,	25
Fried, crumbs or batter	25
Chowder,	15

LITTLE NECKS:

Dozen,	20
Half-Dozen,	10
Stewed,	40
Fried,	45
Quahaugs, Stewed,	25
" Fried,	35

SCALLOPS. (in Season.)

Fried,	35
Stewed,	30

Crackers and Milk,	15
Bread and Milk,	15
Dry Toast,	10
Buttered Toast,	10
Milk Toast,	15
Boiled Eggs, (3)	20
Fried Eggs, 3)	20
Dropped Eggs, (3)	20
Eggs on Toast,	20
Bread and Butter,	5
Extra Crackers,	5

Apple Pie,	5
Mince "	5
Lemon "	5
Squash "	5
Custard"	5

Tea,	5
Coffee,	5
Milk,	5
Ginger Ale, (Pureoxia)	5
Sarsaparilla,	5

PLEASE PAY THE WAITER.

Menu from Atwood & Bacon, as the Union Oyster House was known in 1846

Today, the Union Oyster House's menu still offers great oysters and clams—stewed, fried, roasted, and on the half shell—but there are more than two dozen seafood entrées available, including six lobster dishes. Atwood & Bacon's customers would no doubt have been surprised—or appalled—to see lobster on the menu as it was not considered a delicacy but instead "poverty food," a cheap source of protein fed mostly to indentured servants and laborers. In fact, in Massachusetts, a group of servants rebelled and had it written in their contracts that they could not be fed lobster more than three times a week.

In addition to the wide range of good, old-fashioned New England dishes, the Union Oyster House offers steaks and chops, famous cornbread and baked beans, a children's menu, and classic desserts such as Indian Pudding, Apple Cobbler, Gingerbread, and, of course, Boston Cream Pie. As the Milanos will tell you, it's not haute cuisine; it's just great classic New England fare. And they plan to keep it that way. After all, it's an approach that has kept people coming year after year. As Joe Milano, a fourth-generation Bostonian, says: "We New Englanders are simple, straightforward people who love our fresh fish and our food simple and to the point. That's why our basic menu stays the same. We use recipes that have been handed down for generations. There is continuity in keeping with our long history."

And the Milanos value continuity among the people who work at the Union Oyster House.

Since the Union Oyster House opened its doors in 1826, it has been in possession of only four families. The Atwoods were the first owners. After eighty-seven years, the Atwoods sold the business to the Fitzgerald family. They in turn sold the business to the Greaves, who operated the Union Oyster House until 1970 when the Milanos took over.

When you come in the front door, on the left are the stars of the Union Oyster House show: the shuckers behind the semicircular bar. Take a stool and be treated to not only the freshest clams and

HALF DOZEN OYSTERS 4⁸
CLAMS HALF   DOZ
CHERRYSTONES $4⁵⁰
LITTLE NECKS $4⁵⁰

CLAM CHOWDER Sm 8⁰
CLAM CHOWDER LG $2⁵⁰
GLASS OF WINE $2⁷⁵
BEER & ALE ON TAP
                 2²⁵

THE FREEDOM TRAIL
BOSTON

Est. 1826

StanKotzen '03

oysters on the half shell, but to entertainment. John Ferarri has been at the Union Oyster House for thirty-six years. When asked what the best part of his job is, he jokes, "When they lock the door!" He then says: "It's definitely the customers and getting to talk to so many different people. And to educate people about shellfish."

As you sit at the oyster bar, you may be served some still-warm house-made potato chips and get to see John and his colleague, Anton Christen, entertain their guests. And it's a floor show that everyone can enjoy—whether it's watching John "train" a lobster, show a group from Texas how to hold a lobster without getting pinched, or tell people they are "sitting in [U.S. Senator and former presidential candidate] John Kerry's seat," there's never a dull moment.

Staff who put in many long years of service is nothing new at the Union Oyster House. Rose Carey, the first waitress in Boston, worked there for sixty years. Jim Farren, better known as "Pop," shucked oysters at the bar for sixty-five years, starting somewhere around 1869. Tommy Butt shucked oysters until 1985, when he retired shortly after his eightieth birthday. He had been at the Union Oyster House for fifty-two years.

"The Union Oyster House has been a cathedral, or more properly speaking a chapel, of seafood, its high altar the oyster bar, its acolytes and priests the white-coated experts who render available and edible its Cotuits and Little Necks, its worshippers the patrons whose mouths water and whose nostrils quiver at the salt odor of lobster broiling on a coal fire in its kitchens."
—*Codfish Cathedral*, by Lucius Beebe,
New York Herald Tribune, September 27th, 1931

Behind the scenes, more than thirty-five people—chefs, prep cooks, and kitchen workers—keep things running smoothly in the three kitchens (plus a bakery) that produce the restaurant's classic dishes, serving as many as 1,500 meals a day.

As Bill Coyne, the executive chef who has been managing this mammoth undertaking since January 1, 2000, says: "An operation this big always has something to keep you interested. It's not fancy food; it's just great fresh New England food that keeps people coming back and brings in visitors from all over the world." As a native Bostonian with a degree in history, Bill says: "It was an automatic fit. And I knew the Milanos' reputation—they were a big part of my decision to come on board."

The challenges of running a large restaurant are numerous, but on top of that, when you are working in a National Historic Landmark, great care has to be taken with even the simplest upgrades and maintenance in order to preserve the integrity of the building. Simple matters such as replacing a window can involve an architect as well as a preservationist. In a sense, the Milanos and their extended Union Oyster House family are curators of a living—and very lively—museum.

According to Bill, every year, the staff serves some 60,000 plates of oysters on the half shell. That doesn't include oysters served stuffed, broiled, scalloped, or in stews. All told, the Union Oyster House goes through more than 750,000 oysters and 60,000 pounds of lobsters a year.

The Neighborhood

While Daniel Webster would recognize the interior of the Union Oyster House, the neighborhood would not be familiar. In those days, the building was on the Boston waterfront. While none of Boston is far from the ocean, the back door of the building opened onto the wharves, making it convenient to unload cargo. The area where the Union Oyster House is now boasts some of the oldest buildings in the city and is part of the route of the famous Freedom Trail.

Nearby is bustling Faneuil Hall, with its great shops and restaurants. There are one hundred shops and carts, and forty restaurants within Faneuil Hall Marketplace. Faneuil Hall

The building when it was known as At the Sign of the Cornfields

Marketplace comprises four places at one location—Faneuil Hall, Quincy Market, North Market, and South Market. Faneuil Hall itself was built in 1742 as both a commercial and civic center, and was a hotbed of Revolutionary activity. It was here that the doctrine of "no taxation without representation" was established and later George Washington toasted the new country's first birthday. In 1826, Faneuil Hall was expanded to include the Quincy Market. The entire area was renovated in the 1970s and today receives more than 18 million visitors every year.

After Quincy Market opened in 1974, Boston went from being number fifty-nine on the list of U.S. cities to visit, to number six. The addition of a new convention center, with the distinction of being closer to a major airport than any other convention center in the country, helped hotel occupancy rise from 275,000 people to 650,000 a year. Boston remains a small, safe, and cultural city—easily walkable and user-friendly for visitors.

The History of the
Union Oyster House

The Brick Building on Union Street:
A Look Back in Time

According to the plaque presented to the Union Oyster House in 2003 designating it a National Historic Landmark, the Union Oyster House is not only the oldest continually operated restaurant in the country but "the earliest building constructed between 1716 and 1717 located within the Blackstone block and is the earliest standing brick building in Boston." This much is known. But the earliest history of the site is a little vague: detailed historic records simply don't go back that far. Boston was beginning to be settled as early as 1630. Before the construction of the brick building that is now the Union Oyster House, it's believed that in 1657 a multitasker by the name of William Courser (or Cosser, perhaps) owned an inn and a cobbler's shop on the same site, while moonlighting as the first town crier of Boston. The earliest deeds on record show that John Sawell purchased the property in 1713. It then changed hands four times, at which point Thomas Stoddard bought the property. His daughter Patience Stoddard Capen and her husband Hopestill Capen inherited the property and opened a dry goods store, known as At the Sign of the Cornfields.

A Revolutionary Tide: The Years of Intrigue

At this point, the site's history begins to get interesting. By 1769 Patience and Hopestill were keeping shop, along with a clerk by the name of Benjamin Thompson, who was sixteen years old at the time. About two years later, a publisher by the name of Isaiah

The Freedom Trail

The Freedom Trail, an atmospheric 2 1/2-mile walk from Boston Common to the Bunker Hill Monument, is one of the most popular historic walks in the country. You can start anywhere along the trail and linger at any of the sixteen intriguing sites:

1. The Boston Common. America's oldest public park, originally a common grazing ground, is now home to numerous outdoor events.

2. The State House. The "new" State House was completed in 1798 and widely acclaimed as one of the more magnificent buildings in the country. It sits on land formerly owned by John Hancock who used it as a cow pasture.

3. Park Street Church. Founded in 1809, the Park Street Church has a history of social activism, serving as a forum for the Abolitionist movement, prison reform, and women's suffrage.

4. Granary Burying Ground. Among those buried in this beautiful cemetery are Paul Revere, Samuel Adams, John Hancock and his servant Frank, as well as Benjamin Franklin's parents.

5. King's Chapel and King's Chapel Burying Ground. Completed in 1754 and designed by Peter Harrison, America's first architect, the interior of the chapel is considered by many to be the finest example of Georgian church architecture in North America. Paul Revere crafted King Chapel's 2,347-pound bell in 1816, deeming it the "sweetest sounding" he had ever created. The King's Chapel Burying Ground is even older than the Granary Burying Ground. Note Joseph Tapping's headstone in the front of the cemetery where the Grim Reaper and Father Time battle over the eventuality of death.

6. Benjamin Franklin Statue/Boston Latin School. Boston Latin School was the first public school in America. It continues today in the Fenway section of the city.

7. Old Corner Book Store. This was the original home of the Atlantic Monthly and Ticknor & Fields, which published the works of Henry Wadsworth Longfellow, Harriet Beecher Stowe, Nathaniel Hawthorne, Ralph Waldo Emerson, Charles Dickens, and Louisa May Alcott.

8. Old South Meeting House. Originally a Puritan church, the meetinghouse figured largely in the Revolution and was the starting point for the Boston Tea Party.

9. Old State House. This was the seat of British government during the Revolution. After the Revolution, it became the Commonwealth's first State House until the new one was completed in 1798.

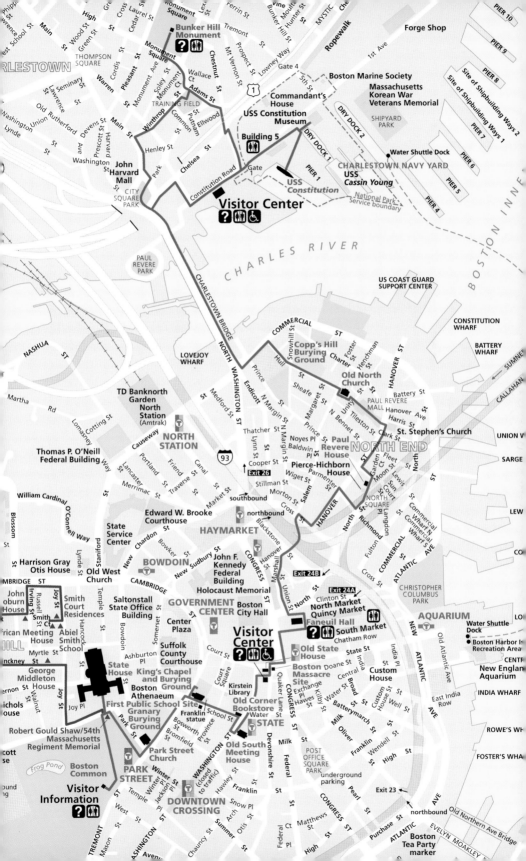

10. Site of the Boston Massacre. This took place outside the Old State House. In 1770, British soldiers fired on rebellious colonists, the first deadly skirmish of the impending war. The British soldiers were tried for murder, but the incident became a rallying cry for the revolutionaries.

11. Faneuil Hall. Only a few blocks from the Union Oyster House, this was built in 1741 and was a marketplace, town hall, and center of the Revolution. Today Faneuil Hall Marketplace (which encompasses Faneuil Hall, Quincy Market, North Market, and South Market) houses more than one hundred shops and vending carts as well as forty restaurants.

12. Paul Revere House. Located about one-half mile north of Faneuil Hall, this is the only home on the Freedom Trail. Paul Revere and his family were living there when he made his famous midnight ride.

13. The Old North Church. On April 18, 1775, from the steeple of the Old North Church, sexton Robert Newman held high two lanterns as a signal from Paul Revere that the British were marching to Lexington and Concord to arrest Samuel Adams and John Hancock, and to seize the colonial store of ammunition. These were the events that ignited the American Revolution.

14. Copp's Hill Burying Ground. Buried here are colonial preachers Cotton and Increase Mather, and sexton Robert Newman. The grounds are also the final resting place of close to one thousand free African Americans who lived nearby in the New Guinea Community.

15. U.S.S. Constitution ("Old Ironsides") & U.S.S. Constitution Museum. Across the Charles River is the *U.S.S. Constitution*, the oldest commissioned warship in the world. It was nicknamed Old Ironsides in the War of 1812 when cannonballs were seen bouncing off its sides.

16. Bunker Hill Monument. This 221-foot obelisk marks the site of the first major battle of the Revolution in which Colonel William Prescott is said to have instructed the troops, "Don't fire until you see the whites of their eyes!"

The Union Oyster House is located along the route of the famous Freedom Trail, near Faneuil Hall Marketplace, stop number twelve on the trail.

Across the street from the Union Oyster House is a memorial that pays tribute to a more recent period in history: the New England Holocaust Memorial. Designed by Stanley Saitowitz and dedicated in 1995, six luminous 54-foot-tall glass towers are inscribed with the names of the six million people who were victims of the Holocaust. Haunting and beautiful, it's impossible not to be moved by the sight of it.

Thomas moved into the building on Union Street and began publishing the *Massachusetts Spy*, a name that, at the time, had no particular connotation of revolutionary leanings. It was simply the name of the newspaper, with a motto that read "Open to all parties, but influenced by none." It was, however, funded by John Hancock. Isaiah had been fired from a job at the *Halifax Gazette* in Nova Scotia, Canada, for his strong opposition to the Stamp Act, a tax imposed by the British government in 1765 on all printed materials, from licenses to playing cards.

So it came as no surprise that Isaiah soon felt the pull of revolutionary fervor, and the *Massachusetts Spy* became one of the most outspoken critics of Britain and an important force in the struggle

The Union Street building has had many tenants including the *Massachusetts Spy*, an anti-British Revolutionary War newspaper.

Toothpick Anyone?

In the late 1800s, the wooden toothpick was first introduced to the public at the Union Oyster House in response to "consumer demand." In fact, inventor Charles Forster—inspired by time spent in South America where he saw people cleaning their teeth with a small sliver of wood—developed a toothpick machine using birch wood from Maine. But business wasn't good. Unable to convince restaurant owners that toothpicks would catch on with customers, legend has it that Charles got a handful of hard-up Harvard students to dine at the Union Oyster House and then demand toothpicks after the meal (in exchange for Charles picking up the tab). When told that there weren't any toothpicks, the students agreed to complain loudly and threaten never to return. From then on, toothpicks were made available. They caught on in other Boston establishments and eventually in other parts of the country.

for independence. So much so that Isaiah relocated to Worcester in 1775 in order to avoid British hostility. Early that year, a rebellious colonist who had been stripped, tarred, and feathered was paraded by the British in front of the *Spy* office where some of the soldiers were said to have announced that "the printer of the *Spy* shall be the next to receive this punishment." Isaiah's press would later become known as the Sedition Foundry.

But these were volatile times. The following year, Hopestill Capen, the owner of the building on Union Street, was jailed for his loyalty to the Crown. He wrote an impassioned letter that same year defending his rights, a document that survives to this day and was auctioned to a collector in 2006 for nearly $9,000.

Along with the *Massachusetts Spy*, also housed in the Union Street building, was an actual British spy: none other than Benjamin Thompson, the Capen's clerk. Benjamin's activities from 1773 to 1775 were so useful to the British government that when he went to England as a bearer of dispatches, he returned as under-secretary of the colonies in 1780. When he returned again to England in 1783, he was rewarded with the title of Count Rumford. During his time as a spy on Union Street, there is some evidence that he pioneered the use of invisible ink. If only walls could talk!

Not only was this building a hotbed of intrigue, it served as the headquarters of Continental Army paymaster Ebenezer Hancock, John Hancock's rather less distinguished brother. The pay, when available, came courtesy of France, which supported the colonists' revolutionary cause.

At long last, the war ended in 1783 with a victory for the Continental Army under the generalship of George Washington, who took his oath of office as the first president in 1789.

Timeline for the Site of the Union Oyster House
Here is a brief look at the history of the Union Street building.

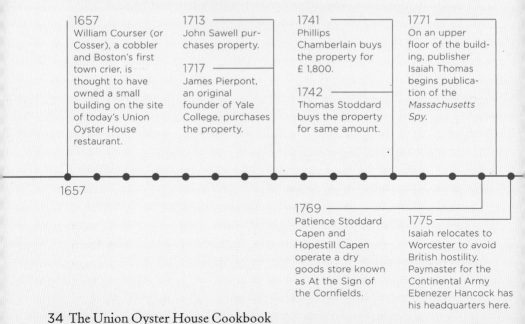

1657
William Courser (or Cosser), a cobbler and Boston's first town crier, is thought to have owned a small building on the site of today's Union Oyster House restaurant.

1713
John Sawell purchases property.

1717
James Pierpont, an original founder of Yale College, purchases the property.

1741
Phillips Chamberlain buys the property for £ 1,800.

1742
Thomas Stoddard buys the property for same amount.

1771
On an upper floor of the building, publisher Isaiah Thomas begins publication of the *Massachusetts Spy*.

1657

1769
Patience Stoddard Capen and Hopestill Capen operate a dry goods store known as At the Sign of the Cornfields.

1775
Isaiah relocates to Worcester to avoid British hostility. Paymaster for the Continental Army Ebenezer Hancock has his headquarters here.

Landlords to the Future King of France

Hopestill and Patience continued to operate the store, importing fancy dress goods and silks from England and Paris. It may well have been through this French connection that the Duc de Chartres came to live in the building on Union Street in 1797, living in exile after the French Revolution began to spin out of control. Even though Louis Phillippe was a liberal, and sympathized with the philosophy of government by the people and not by the divine right of kings, he was at risk. His father was guillotined, and Louis Philippe left the country, wandering in exile for years. Some of this time, he spent in Boston, in none other than the upper floors of the brick building on Union Street. There he met important and influential Americans, as well as taught French and, some say, dancing to the upper-crust jeune filles of Boston. He eventually returned to France where he became known as "the citizen king" and

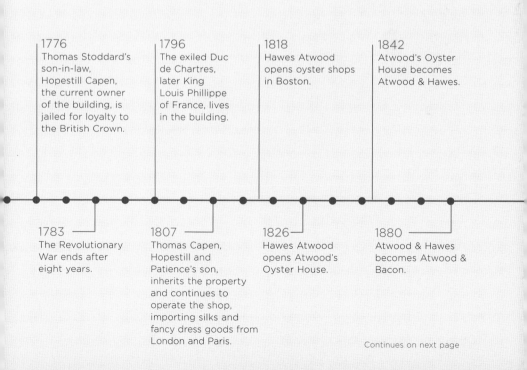

1776
Thomas Stoddard's son-in-law, Hopestill Capen, the current owner of the building, is jailed for loyalty to the British Crown.

1796
The exiled Duc de Chartres, later King Louis Phillippe of France, lives in the building.

1818
Hawes Atwood opens oyster shops in Boston.

1842
Atwood's Oyster House becomes Atwood & Hawes.

1783
The Revolutionary War ends after eight years.

1807
Thomas Capen, Hopestill and Patience's son, inherits the property and continues to operate the shop, importing silks and fancy dress goods from London and Paris.

1826
Hawes Atwood opens Atwood's Oyster House.

1880
Atwood & Hawes becomes Atwood & Bacon.

Continues on next page

the "bourgeois monarch" until he faced another rebellion and was again forced into exile.

Thomas Capen, Patience and Hopestill's son, inherited the building in 1807 and continued in the family business until his death in 1819.

And Then Came the Oysters

It was in 1826 that an oyster house opened on Union Street. Hawes Atwood, whose family had other oyster houses in Boston, opened the Union Street restaurant as Atwood's Oyster House. The restaurant became Atwood & Hawes from approximately 1842 to 1860 and then Atwood & Bacon from the late 1800s to 1916 when it became known as the Union Oyster House.

After eighty-seven years in business, the Atwood family sold the restaurant in 1913 to the Fitzgerald family who owned the property until at least 1927. The Greaves brothers of Nova Scotia

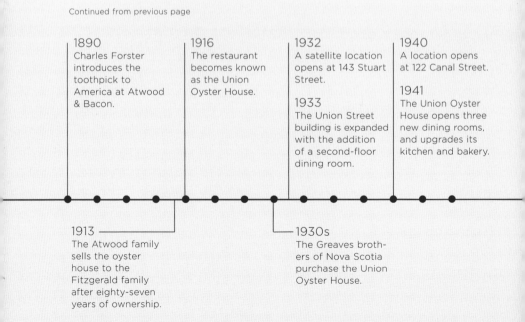

Continued from previous page

1890
Charles Forster introduces the toothpick to America at Atwood & Bacon.

1916
The restaurant becomes known as the Union Oyster House.

1932
A satellite location opens at 143 Stuart Street.

1933
The Union Street building is expanded with the addition of a second-floor dining room.

1940
A location opens at 122 Canal Street.

1941
The Union Oyster House opens three new dining rooms, and upgrades its kitchen and bakery.

1913
The Atwood family sells the oyster house to the Fitzgerald family after eighty-seven years of ownership.

1930s
The Greaves brothers of Nova Scotia purchase the Union Oyster House.

owned the property by 1940 and began to operate satellite branches in other parts of town. The restaurant itself had been expanded in 1933 when a second-floor dining room opened with seating for fifty. In 1941, the oyster house opened three new dining rooms on the second floor and installed a new kitchen and bakery with all new cooking and dishwashing equipment. The Greaves sold the restaurant in 1970 to Joseph Milano Sr., whose family continues to run the renowned Union Oyster House today.

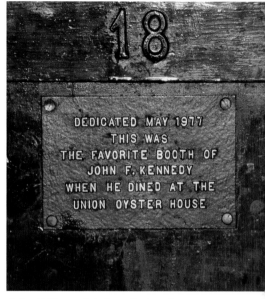

John F. Kennedy's favorite booth, Number 18

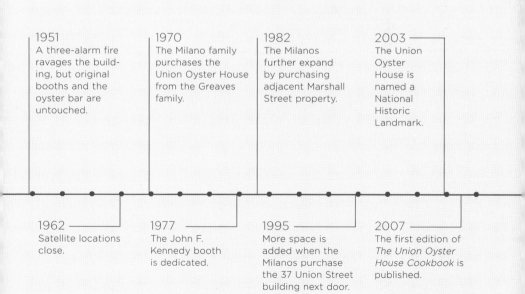

1951
A three-alarm fire ravages the building, but original booths and the oyster bar are untouched.

1970
The Milano family purchases the Union Oyster House from the Greaves family.

1982
The Milanos further expand by purchasing adjacent Marshall Street property.

2003
The Union Oyster House is named a National Historic Landmark.

1962
Satellite locations close.

1977
The John F. Kennedy booth is dedicated.

1995
More space is added when the Milanos purchase the 37 Union Street building next door.

2007
The first edition of *The Union Oyster House Cookbook* is published.

Who Was Daniel Webster?

There has been no end of famous people—including John F. Kennedy, Meryl Streep, and Tiger Woods—who have enjoyed the Union Oyster House, but Daniel Webster has a place to himself (possibly because of his remarkable appetite for oysters). He was a regular patron of the Oyster House and would frequently sit down to three dozen oysters washed down by several tumblers of brandy.

Like the Kennedys and Senator John Kerry, Daniel Webster was a native son of Massachusetts, even if he did start out in New Hampshire. Daniel was a U.S. senator for Massachusetts from 1827 to 1841 and again from 1845 to 1850. He also served as secretary of state and often was considered as a potential candidate for president. He is now probably best known as a great orator both within the Senate and as a public speaker, giving a famous speech on the deaths of Thomas Jefferson and John Adams. Daniel Webster's statue stands in front of the State House on the Freedom Trail.

In 1982, the Milanos expanded the restaurant by purchasing the adjacent Marshall Street property, and in 1995, the site expanded again with the addition of the 37 Union Street building. In 2003, the Union Oyster House was designated a National Historic Landmark.

Appetizers

Naturally, the Union Oyster House is best known for its oysters on the half shell, serving more than 60,000 plates every year. But be sure to try some of the other delicacies on the half shell, such as cherrystones and littlenecks. Or, order a Cold Seafood Sampler that includes some of each along with chilled shrimp. Hot appetizers include classics such as Oysters Rockefeller and Clams Casino, a New England favorite. A Hot Seafood Sampler is also on the menu.

Oysters on the Half Shell

Watching the star oyster shuckers behind the original semicircular bar at the Union Oyster House is one of the best parts of a visit to America's oldest restaurant. You may never develop the speed that John, Anton, and the others have, but once you get the hang of it, you'll be able to enjoy the incomparable briny flavor of oysters on the half shell at home.

1. Working at a comfortable counter height, place the oyster—with the deeper side of the shell facing down—on a folded kitchen towel to prevent it from slipping. Fold part of the towel over the oyster to protect your hand from any jagged edges while holding the oyster.

2. Insert the blunt point of an oyster knife into the hinge of the oyster shell.

   Firmly apply pressure downward while slightly twisting your wrist to pry the shells apart. The shells will eventually pop and separate.

3. Slide your knife under the oyster to loosen it (be careful to reserve the oyster juice inside the shell).

4. Discard the top shell and serve immediately with your favorite sauce.

Shucking oysters at today's Union Oyster House

Classic Cocktail Sauce

When you order oysters at the bar at the Union Oyster House, you can mix your own cocktail sauce to taste with ketchup, hot sauce, lemon, and horseradish.

1 cup ketchup

1 1/2 tablespoons prepared
  horseradish, or to taste

3 tablespoons lemon juice

Hot sauce and Worcestershire
  sauce, to taste

1. Combine all ingredients. Chill well.

2. Serve with oysters or clams on the half shell or with your favorite chilled seafood.

Makes 1 1/4 cups

Mignonette Sauce

This is a classic French sauce preferred by some oyster purists. It really does let the oyster flavor shine. Essentially, you are pickling minced shallots, so make the sauce at least a couple of hours before you serve it. Invest in a good-quality vinegar—this will be smoother than a less expensive one.

1 large shallot, minced

1/2 teaspoon freshly ground
  black pepper

1/2 cup red wine vinegar

1/2 cup dry sherry

1 teaspoon chopped chives or
  minced parsley

1. Combine all ingredients. Chill well before serving.

Makes 1 cup

The Oyster Family

Although oysters go by a variety of names, there are only four actual varieties. These are spread over such a wide range of coastline that they develop distinctive local tastes and textures.

Eastern Oysters are also known as Bluepoints (Long Island), Malpeque (Prince Edward Island), Chincoteague (Virginia), Breton Sound (Louisiana), Wellfleet (Massachusetts), and Cotuit (Nantucket), among others. The oysters from the colder waters of the North Atlantic are usually firmer and somewhat brinier in taste. They are perfectly good eaten year-round, although some feel that in the summer months, these oysters are softer and less tangy when they are spawning—hence the old adage that oysters are best enjoyed in months with an r, i.e., September through April.

The oysters served at the Union Oyster House are all northern, cold water varieties. They come from Wellfleet, a Cape Cod town famous for its oysters, or from Duxbury, Massachusetts; Bluepoints come from Connecticut and Long Island.

Union Special Oysters

This is a classic—and delicious—oyster preparation that has been on the menu at the Union Oyster House for decades. It appeared on a 1930s menu as "Broiled Oysters on Half Shell, Union Special, Half Dozen" for 45 cents! A small serving of oyster stew was 30 cents.

1/4 cup butter
3 slices bacon, diced
1/2 cup diced green pepper
1/2 cup diced red pepper
1/2 cup minced onion
1 cup chopped mushrooms
1 clove garlic, minced
1/3 cup clam juice
Dash hot sauce, to taste
Dash Worcestershire sauce,
   to taste
Salt and black pepper, to taste
1/2 cup crushed potato chips
1/4 cup bread crumbs
   (more if needed)
12 oysters, freshly shucked
   on the half shell
Grated Parmesan cheese,
   as needed
6 lemon wedges, for garnish

1. Preheat oven to 450°F. In a saucepan, melt the butter. Sauté the bacon in the butter until it is rendered and crispy. Remove and drain on paper towels. Add the peppers, onion, mushrooms, and garlic, and cook until vegetables are soft and mushrooms have given up their liquid.

2. Add clam juice and bring to a boil. Add hot sauce, Worcestershire sauce, salt, and black pepper. Add potato chips and bread crumbs and stir until almost all of the liquid is absorbed.

3. Place oysters on the half shell on a baking sheet and place a spoonful of stuffing over each oyster. Sprinkle with Parmesan cheese. Bake 15–20 minutes, or until tops are bubbled and brown. Serve immediately with fresh lemon wedges.

Serves 4–6 as an appetizer

"He was a bold man that first ate an oyster."
—Jonathan Swift

Oysters Rockefeller

Thought to have originated at Antoine's in New Orleans, this is another classic oyster dish. Although the original Antoine's recipe remains a secret, this recipe has been developed by the Union Oyster House chefs and offers a wonderful combination of flavors. Some say it was given its name because it's so rich.

1 pound fresh spinach, cooked, squeezed, and chopped (or 1/2 pound thawed frozen chopped spinach, squeezed dry)

1/2 cup grated Parmesan cheese, plus more for sprinkling

1 tablespoon Dijon mustard

1/2 cup Fish Velouté (see recipe on page 74)

Salt and pepper, to taste

12 oysters, freshly shucked on the half shell

1 cup Hollandaise sauce (see recipe on page 74)

1. Preheat oven to 450°F. In a bowl, combine spinach, cheese, mustard, and velouté. Season to taste with salt and pepper, and stir well to combine.

2. Place oysters on a baking sheet. Place a spoonful of spinach mixture over each oyster. Sprinkle additional Parmesan on top. Bake 10–12 minutes, or until oysters are heated through and the sauce is bubbling.

3. Top each oyster with a teaspoon of warm Hollandaise Sauce.

Serves 4 as an appetizer

Scalloped Oysters

This is a classic preparation that first rose to popularity in the 1800s, especially as a part of holiday feasts.

1 tablespoon melted butter

1 teaspoon minced garlic

2 tablespoons white wine

1 cup heavy cream

1/2 teaspoon Dijon mustard

Pinch dried thyme

12 oysters, freshly shucked on the half shell

1/4 cup seasoned bread crumbs

1. Preheat broiler. In a skillet, heat the butter and garlic until sizzling. Add the white wine to the pan and stir.

2. Add the heavy cream, mustard, and thyme. Bring to a boil, then reduce heat and simmer until the mixture reduces by about one half and becomes thick.

3. Lift oysters from their shells and line shells with about 1 teaspoon of crumbs.

4. Spoon about 1 teaspoon of the cream sauce over the crumbs. Place each oyster back in its shell. Spoon another teaspoon of sauce over each oyster.

5. Broil until browned and bubbly, about 3–4 minutes.

Serves 4 as an appetizer

Clams on the Half Shell

Like oysters, these take a little practice to open but are well worth the effort.

1. Rinse any sand or grit off the outside of the shell and allow the clams to rest for half an hour or so. If they are undisturbed, the shell seal may be a bit more relaxed.

2. Hold a clam in one hand, preferably using a heavy glove, and work a clam knife between the shells opposite the hinged end.

3. Once the knife is between the shells, turn it to pry them open. Use the knife to detach the clam from the top and bottom shells. Discard one of the shells and place the clam in the other to serve.

4. Like oysters, these can be served with Mignonette Sauce or Classic Cocktail Sauce. (See page 44 for recipes.)

Know Your Clams

East Coast clams fall into two major categories: hard shell and soft shell. Hard-shell clams—which are served raw on the half shell, stuffed, or in chowders—are classified by size. Quahogs are the largest and are sometimes used for chowders or stuffed clams; but they are a mouthful to be eaten raw. Next are midsized cherrystones, named for Cherrystone Creek in Virginia. Littlenecks, named for Littleneck Bay on Long Island, are the smallest. Only the more delicate littlenecks and cherrystones that come from Cape Cod (not quahogs) are served at the Union Oyster House.

Soft-shell clams are most often used for steaming (in fact, they are also known as "steamers") and are usually served this way with melted butter, but they also make for great fried clams. Ipswich clams, the gold standard in New England, are the only ones served at the Union Oyster House.

Clams Casino

Thought to be an 1800s creation of Julius Keller, maître d' at the seaside casino in Narragansett, Rhode Island, this is now a familiar eastern seaboard favorite.

1/2 cup butter or margarine
2 tablespoons diced green pepper
2 tablespoons diced red pepper or pimento
2 tablespoons diced onion
Hot sauce and Worcestershire sauce, to taste
12 littleneck clams, freshly opened on the half shell
4 slices bacon, cut into 3 pieces each

1. Preheat oven to 350°F. Place the butter, peppers, pimento, and onion in a mixing bowl and blend thoroughly by hand until the butter is softened and all the ingredients are incorporated.

2. Mix in the hot sauce and Worcestershire sauce.

3. Place a spoonful of the topping on each clam and top with a piece of bacon.

4. Bake 5–7 minutes, or until the clams are heated through and the bacon is crisp.

Serves 4 as an appetizer

Baked Stuffed Cherrystone Clams (or Oysters)

These are a wonderful, savory introduction to any meal. They also make a good lunch or supper dish with a green salad and some crusty bread.

1 1/2 tablespoons butter
2 tablespoons diced onion
2 tablespoons diced green pepper
2 tablespoons chopped mushrooms
1/4 teaspoon white pepper
1/4 teaspoon mustard powder
1/4 teaspoon garlic powder
1/4 teaspoon oregano
2 tablespoons clam juice
1/4 cup water
Bread crumbs, as needed (about 1/2 cup)
12 cherrystone clams, freshly opened on the half shell

1. Preheat oven to 350°F. Melt the butter in a skillet until it begins to sizzle. Add the onion, peppers, and mushrooms, and cook until the onions are translucent and the liquid from the mushrooms has cooked away.

2. Add the seasonings, clam juice, and water and bring to a boil.

3. Remove from the heat and add enough bread crumbs to form a stuffing. Allow to cool.

4. Place clams on a baking sheet. Stuff each clam with a spoonful of the filling and bake 10–12 minutes, until heated through. Serve immediately.

Serves 4 as an appetizer

Steamed Mussels, Basque Style

There are very good farmed mussels that are widely available, and these tend to be plumper than the wild ones. Mussels have been part of the European diet for ages, but have only really become popular in the United States within the last ten years. This is a classic Spanish preparation.

1 1/4 pounds mussels
1 cup clam juice
1/2 cup white wine
1 tablespoon chopped garlic
2 tablespoons chopped onion
1 tablespoon chopped parsley
Garlic bread, for serving

1. Place all ingredients in a 2-quart saucepan and bring to a boil. Reduce heat and simmer, covered, until the mussels open, about 5 minutes.

2. Pour mussels into a large bowl or crock and serve with garlic bread for dipping.

Serves 2 as an appetizer

Soups, Chowders, and Stews

Seafood chowders, soups, and stews are an essential part of New England cuisine. Every seafaring culture has its own version, but many New England dishes are characterized by the addition of milk, although this didn't come about until the mid-1800s. The earliest seafood soups were probably made on board fishing boats, where, in addition to fresh fish, you might well have had salt pork, crackers, onions, and potatoes in the galley (as they all keep well). Milk would have been a luxury. But gradually, as availability increased and refrigeration became common, New England chowders became characteristically milk-based.

Oyster Stew

This recipe hasn't changed much since the Union Oyster House first opened. It's been an important holiday dish in New England since the 1800s. As James Wiles wrote in Philadelphia's *Bulletin:* "My gold standard for oyster stew . . . is the version served at the Union Oyster House in Boston. The Union's oyster stew is made with nothing more than heavy cream, butter, and oysters. A glass of wine, a few hard oyster crackers, and all is bliss."

1 pint half-and-half, milk, or heavy cream—or a combination
2 tablespoons butter
16 raw oysters, freshly shucked, with their juices
Paprika or finely chopped parsley
Salt, pepper, Worcestershire sauce, and hot sauce, to taste

1. Scald the half-and-half, milk, or cream by heating it until a thin skin forms on top.

2. In a saucepan, melt the butter over low heat. Add the oysters and their juices to the pan and sauté until plumped.

3. Combine the cream, and butter and oyster mixture in a crock or soup bowl.

4. Season to taste with salt, pepper, Worcestershire sauce, and hot sauce. Sprinkle with paprika or parsley and serve hot.

Serves 4

Fish Chowder

The word chowder is thought to come from the French word *chaudiere*, or cauldron. This was the pot that Gallic fishermen used to cook their seafood soups and stews. There are good premade fish stocks in the grocery store if you don't have time to make your own.

1/4 cup diced salt pork
2 tablespoons butter
1/2 cup diced onion
1/2 cup diced celery
2 tablespoons flour
1/2 teaspoon dried thyme
2 cups peeled and
  diced potatoes
2 cups fish stock
1 1/2 pounds cod, cut into
  chunks
1 cup half-and-half
Salt, pepper, hot sauce,
  and Worcestershire sauce,
  to taste.

1. In a large pot over medium-low heat, render the salt pork until it is crispy, about 5 minutes.

2. Add the butter to the pan. When melted, add onion and celery, and cook until onion is translucent, about 5 minutes. Stir in the flour to form a paste and cook, stirring constantly, for 2–3 minutes.

3. Add the thyme, potatoes, and fish stock, and bring to a boil, stirring almost constantly. Reduce heat and simmer 10 minutes, until potatoes are tender.

4. Add the cod and bring quickly to a boil, stirring almost constantly.

5. Add the half-and-half and bring quickly to a boil. Season with salt, pepper, hot sauce, and Worcestershire sauce. Serve immediately.

Makes 1 1/2 quarts

Clam Chowder

This is the quintessential New England clam chowder. There are two other versions: Manhattan, which is tomato-based, and Rhode Island, which is similar to the recipe below but doesn't include the cream. Die-hard New Englanders consider these other varieties an affront.

1/4 cup diced salt pork
2 tablespoons butter
1/2 cup diced onion
1/2 cup diced celery
2 tablespoons flour
1/2 teaspoon dried thyme
2 cups peeled and diced
  potatoes
2 cups canned clam juice
2 cups minced fresh or frozen
  clams (not canned)
1 cup half-and-half
Salt, pepper, hot sauce, and
  Worcestershire sauce,
  to taste

1. In a large pot over medium-low heat, render the salt pork until it is crispy, about 5 minutes.

2. Add the butter, and melt. Add onion and celery, and cook until translucent, about 5 minutes. Stir in the flour to form a paste and cook, stirring constantly, for 2–3 minutes.

3. Add the thyme, potatoes, and clam juice, and bring to a boil, stirring almost constantly. Reduce heat and simmer 10 minutes, until potatoes are tender.

4. Add the clams and bring quickly to a boil, stirring almost constantly.

5. Add the half-and-half and bring quickly to a boil. Season with salt, pepper, hot sauce, and Worcestershire sauce. Serve immediately.

Makes 1 1/2 quarts

Old-Fashioned Lobster Stew

What could be more Yankee than good old lobster stew?
It's simple and delicious.

2 cups half-and-half
1/4 cup butter
2 cups cooked diced lobster
meat
Salt and pepper, to taste
Minced chives, for garnish

1. Scald the half-and-half by heating it over low heat until a thin skin forms on top.

2. In a skillet, melt the butter. Add the lobster meat and sauté until heated through.

3. Divide lobster meat evenly among four serving bowls. Pour half-and-half over lobster. Season to taste with salt and pepper. Garnish with chives.

Serves 4

Fisherman's Stew

This is a long-standing favorite at the Union Oyster House. It showcases some of New England's most delicious shellfish.

2 cups light cream or
  half-and-half
2 tablespoons butter
1/2 cup soft-shell (steamer)
  clams, freshly shucked
1/2 cup oysters, freshly shucked
4 sea scallops
4 shrimp, peeled and deveined
Salt and pepper, to taste
Paprika or finely chopped
  parsley, for garnish

1. Scald the cream over low heat by heating it until a thin skin forms over the top.

2. Melt the butter in a skillet and sauté all of the seafood until just cooked through. Season to taste with salt and pepper.

3. Divide the seafood evenly between two serving bowls. Ladle the scalded cream over the seafood. Season to taste. Top with paprika or chopped parsley.

Serves 2

American Bouillabaisse

People are very opinionated about bouillabaisse. Some think it can't possibly be made correctly without fish native to the Mediterranean, but these fish stews were probably made from whatever catch the fishermen had at the end of the day. The best dishes are simply made from the best and freshest local ingredients, all included here.

3 tablespoons butter
1 clove garlic, minced
1/2 cup sliced onion
1/2 cup julienned carrot
1/2 cup sliced leeks
Pinch of saffron
1/4 cup white wine
8-ounce can whole tomatoes, coarsely chopped, with their liquid
2 cups fish stock
1-pound cooked lobster, head removed, split in half and then in quarters
2 small cod or haddock fillets (about 4 ounces each)
6–8 mussels, cleaned
4–6 steamer clams or littlenecks, scrubbed
4–6 sea scallops
4 large shrimp, peeled and deveined

1. Heat the butter in a stockpot. Add the garlic, onion, carrot, and leeks, and sauté until vegetables just begin to soften, about 5 minutes.

2. Add the saffron and white wine, and simmer for 5 minutes.

3. Add the tomatoes and simmer 5 minutes more. Add the fish stock and bring to a boil.

4. Add all seafood except shrimp and simmer about 5 minutes, until seafood is just cooked through. Add shrimp and simmer 2–3 minutes longer.

5. Divide the seafood evenly between two serving bowls. Ladle the broth over the seafood. Serve with garlic bread.

Serves 2

"The word is a contraction of two verbs, *bouillir* (to boil) and *abaisser* (to reduce), and in fact bouillabaisse is more a method of rapid cooking than an actual recipe: there are as many versions of 'authentic' bouillabaisses as there are ways of combining fish."
—*Larousse Gastronomique*

Shrimp Bisque

You can use just about any type of shrimp, but if you live in New England, look for northern shrimp in season—from about December to March. It's fairly easy to find shrimp with the heads on, and they are very inexpensive. This isn't essential, but the heads add extra flavor to the stock. Although this dish is somewhat labor intensive, the final product is a delicate bisque that rewards your efforts. It makes a lovely cold-weather lunch or supper with a green salad and crusty bread.

2 pounds northern shrimp,
  heads and shells on
1 cup white wine or dry
  vermouth
2 cups water, divided
1 bay leaf
3 tablespoons butter, divided
1 tablespoon olive oil
1/3 cup chopped celery
1/3 cup chopped shallots

1/3 cup chopped carrots
2 tablespoons flour
2 tablespoons tomato paste
1 teaspoon sea salt
1/2 teaspoon white pepper
1/2 teaspoon Old Bay
  Seasoning
1/4 teaspoon dry mustard
1 pint (2 cups) light cream
2 tablespoons sherry

1. Remove the heads from the shrimp; reserve the heads.

2. Combine the wine and 1 cup of the water in a large pot. Add the bay leaf and bring to a boil. Add the shrimp tails. Reduce the heat and simmer for 2 minutes. Remove the shrimp from the liquid and plunge into cold water to cool. When cool, remove the shells.

3. In the same pot, melt 1 tablespoon of the butter. Add the olive oil, heat through, then add the celery, shallots, and carrots. Sauté until soft, about 7 minutes.

4. Return the shells, the reserved shrimp heads, and the liquid to the pot and simmer over low heat for 20 minutes to make a stock.

5. Strain the liquid though a colander, pressing on the solids.

6. In a saucepan, melt remaining 2 tablespoons of butter over low heat. Whisk in the flour to make a roux. Cook for 4–5 minutes, stirring frequently, being careful not to burn the roux.

7. Whisk in the shrimp stock and simmer over low heat for about 5 minutes, until thick and smooth. Add the tomato paste, salt, pepper, Old Bay Seasoning, and dry mustard.

8. Whisk in the cream and sherry, add the shrimp, and heat through, about one minute. Do not let the soup boil. Serve immediately.

Serves 6-8

Onion Soup

This is the Union Oyster House version of the French classic. The quality of your onion soup is determined by the quality of your beef broth. You can make your own or use a high-quality canned variety.

4 tablespoons vegetable oil

6 cups sliced onions

1/4 cup medium-dry sherry

1 quart beef broth

2–3 bay leaves

1/2 cup grated Romano cheese

6 slices French bread

6 slices Swiss or Gruyere cheese

Black pepper, hot sauce, and Worcestershire sauce, to taste

1. In a large stockpot, heat oil over medium-high heat. Add onions and sauté, stirring occasionally, for 20–25 minutes, until onions have cooked down, and are golden and sweet.

2. Add sherry to deglaze. Add broth and bay leaves, and bring to a boil. Simmer gently for about 1 hour.

3. Remove from heat and stir in Romano cheese.

4. Preheat broiler. Divide soup evenly among six ovenproof soup crocks.

5. Float one slice of baguette in each crock. Lay one slice of cheese over each slice of baguette.

6. Broil soups until cheese is golden brown and bubbly.

Serves 6

Stocks and Sauces

These are some of the building blocks of the Union Oyster House's classic recipes. The two stock recipes can be the basis for all kinds of dishes—soups, chowders, bisques, and sauces. Not only do the stocks provide a flavorful base for any dish you are making, they reflect the traditional economy of Yankee cooking by using leftover fish bones, cuttings, and shells.

Fish Stock

A good fish stock is an essential building block for a variety of seafood chowders, soups, and stews. If you don't want to take the time to make your own, use a high quality canned or bottled fish or clam stock.

2 tablespoons butter

1 small onion, coarsely chopped

2 stalks celery, chopped

6 parsley stems

2 pounds fish bones (from any non-oily white fish)

1 cup white wine

3 quarts water

1. In a large pot, melt butter. Add onion, celery, and parsley stems. Cook, covered, for 5 minutes, stirring occasionally.

2. Add fish bones and cook, covered, for 5 minutes longer.

3. Add white wine and water. Bring to a boil, then reduce heat and simmer half an hour. Strain.

Makes about 3 quarts of stock

Lobster Stock

This can be economical to make if you use the bodies and shells left over from the previous night's lobster feast. If you have lobster when dining out, don't be afraid to ask to take the bodies and shells home.

2 carrots, coarsely chopped
1 onion, coarsely chopped
2 stalks celery, coarsely chopped
1/4 cup tomato purée
1/2 cup white wine
2 pounds lobster bodies and shells
2 sprigs fresh sage
2 sprigs fresh thyme
3 bay leaves
1/4 teaspoon salt
6 whole peppercorns
1 quart water

1. Preheat oven to 375°F. Toss together chopped vegetables and tomato purée. Transfer to a roasting pan and roast for 30 minutes or until lightly browned.

2. Remove roasting pan from oven and place over low heat. Pour white wine over vegetables and use a wooden spoon to loosen vegetables from the bottom of the pan. Transfer vegetables and deglazing liquid to a large stockpot.

3. Add lobster bodies, herbs, salt, peppercorns, and water. Bring to a boil. Reduce heat and simmer 45 minutes. Strain.

Makes about a quart

Fish Velouté

Velouté is a classic French sauce that consists of a butter and flour roux with stock added.

2 tablespoons butter
2 tablespoons flour
1 cup Fish Stock (see recipe on page 72) or clam juice
Salt and pepper, to taste

1. In a small saucepan over medium heat, melt the butter. Stir in the flour and cook 2–3 minutes, stirring constantly, until the mixture is a pale straw color.

2. Whisk in the stock and bring to a boil. Simmer 1–2 minutes, stirring constantly, until thickened. Season with salt and pepper.

Makes 1 cup

Classic Seafood Hollandaise

Don't be intimidated by this classic sauce. It's so good on everything from asparagus to grilled fish, and the blender makes it very easy to prepare.

2 egg yolks
2 teaspoons lemon juice
Pinch salt and pepper
8 tablespoons butter

1. Place the yolks, lemon juice, salt and pepper in a blender.

2. In a small skillet, heat the butter until it is bubbling. With the blender running, pour the butter into the yolk mixture in a thin steady stream until smooth and well blended, about 30–40 seconds. Serve warm.

Makes 1 cup

Café Butter

There are numerous versions of this savory butter that you can use to add flavor to grilled fish, chicken, or meats. The great thing is that you can make it ahead of time, store it in the fridge, and just put a dollop on anything that needs a little extra zest.

1/2 pound butter, softened
1 1/2 tablespoons ketchup
1 tablespoon brandy
1 tablespoon sherry
1 tablespoon minced garlic
1/4 teaspoon each dried parsley, rosemary, basil, and dill
1 tablespoon lemon juice
1 teaspoon lemon zest
Salt and pepper, to taste

1. Blend all ingredients in a food processor. Roll into logs in parchment paper and keep refrigerated.

2. To use, slice off a medallion of butter and place over freshly grilled meat or seafood.

Makes 1 1/2 cups

Creole Sauce

This is a typical New Orleans–style sauce—a tomato base jazzed up with garlic, onion, cayenne pepper, and filé powder. Filé is a powdered form of sassafras root and is used in Cajun cooking to thicken soups, stews, and sauces, and to add a subtle flavor. Our chefs use this on grilled shrimp or as a base for a New Orleans–style seafood stew.

2 tablespoons vegetable oil

2 jalapeños, minced

1 teaspoon crushed red
pepper flakes, or to taste

1 tablespoon garlic

1 cup diced onion

1 cup diced celery

1 cup diced green pepper

2 28-ounce cans crushed
tomatoes

3-ounce can tomato paste

1/2 teaspoon cayenne pepper,
or to taste

2 teaspoons cumin

1 1/2 tablespoons gumbo filé
powder

Salt, to taste

1. In a large, heavy-bottomed stockpot or Dutch oven, heat oil, jalapeños, and red pepper until sizzling.

2. Add garlic and sauté until soft.

3. Add diced vegetables and cook until vegetables begin to soften, about 5 minutes.

4. Add tomatoes, tomato paste, and spices and bring to a boil. Reduce heat and simmer for 1 hour. Add salt to taste.

Makes 1 1/2 quarts

Roasted Red Pepper Sauce

This is terrific with any firm-fleshed grilled or roasted fish, such as swordfish, tuna, or halibut. At the Union Oyster House, the Blackened Shrimp is served with this flavorful sauce.

3-4 large red peppers
1 small red onion, quartered
3 tablespoons olive oil,
  divided
1/2 teaspoon crushed red
  pepper flakes
1 tablespoon minced garlic
1/4 cup red wine
1 pint heavy cream
1 tablespoon tomato purée
2 tablespoons sour cream
Salt and pepper, to taste

1. Preheat oven to 450°F. Toss peppers and onion with 1 tablespoon of the olive oil, place on a baking sheet, and roast for about 20 minutes, until peppers have blistered and onion is golden brown.

2. Remove peppers to a bowl, cover with plastic wrap, and let set about 20 minutes, or until cool enough to handle. Remove skins and seeds, and place in a food processor with roasted onion. Process until smooth. Set aside.

3. In a skillet, sauté crushed red pepper flakes and garlic in remaining 2 tablespoons oil, until garlic begins to brown. Deglaze with red wine and cook for 1 minute.

4. Add puréed red-pepper mixture and simmer 1 minute.

5. Add cream and tomato purée. Bring to a boil, then reduce heat and simmer until mixture reduces by about one-third.

6. Strain sauce and blend in sour cream. Season to taste with salt and pepper. Serve warm with Blackened Shrimp or grilled swordfish or tuna.

Makes 2 cups

Entrées

The great seafood entrées at the Union Oyster House reflect the diversity of American cuisine with French, Cajun, Italian, and, of course, New England influences. You can get as creative as you like with side dishes, but any of these dishes will go well with just a green salad or an asparagus vinaigrette and some crusty bread.

Basic Boiled Lobster

Boiling a lobster is one of the easiest things you can do in the kitchen. All you have to do is watch your timer and make sure the lobsters are bright red when you remove them from the pot. If you are lucky enough to be near clean ocean water, by all means use it to boil your lobster. When you order the Shore Dinner at the Union Oyster House, you also get clam chowder, steamed clams or mussels, corn, potatoes, and dessert—more or less the ingredients of a traditional New England clambake.

6 quarts water

1/2 cup sea salt

4 lively lobsters, 1 1/4 pounds each

1 lemon, cut into 4 wedges, for serving

6 tablespoons melted butter, for serving

1. Bring the water and salt to a boil in a pot large enough to also accommodate the lobsters with ease.

2. Plunge the lobsters into the boiling water headfirst and cover.

3. Boil for approximately 12 minutes.

4. Remove the lobsters from the pot and serve immediately with lemon wedges and/or melted butter.

Serves 4

How to Eat a Lobster

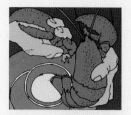

It's amazing how many quirky ways there are to eat a lobster. This is not precisely the way I do it, but this is standard operating procedure. It seems that in New England, everyone has his or her own little tricks and preferences.

1. Put on the bib if you are concerned about getting messy. Don't put on the bib if you are concerned about looking like a tourist. (But the juice can squirt farther than you can believe—as far as across the table—so beware.)

2. Twist off the claws. Crack each claw and knuckle with a lobster cracker or nutcracker. Remove the meat.

3. Separate the tail from the body and break off the tail flippers. Insert a fork (or your finger) and push the tail meat out. You can also crack the tail in half if you need to. Remove and discard the black vein that runs the entire length of the tail meat. You may see bright red coral, or roe, as well as a green substance called the tomalley, or liver. Both are perfectly edible, although their culinary merit is debated. I happen to like both.

4. For smaller lobsters, I don't bother to pick the meat out of the body, but for larger ones, you'll find little pockets of meat where the spindly legs attach to the thorax. Otherwise, just remove the legs and work the meat out of them by pulling them through your front teeth.

5. Use wet napkins to clean yourself—and perhaps your tablemate—up.

Lobster Thermidor

This elegant entrée originated in Paris in 1894. It was created to celebrate the opening of a play by the name of *Thermidor*. The dish stood the test of time far better than its namesake, which closed after a brief run. Dijon mustard gives the sauce its characteristic zip.

2 lobsters, 1 1/4 pounds each
2 tablespoons butter
1/2 cup sliced green pepper
1/2 cup sliced pimentos
1/2 cup sliced mushrooms
2 tablespoons Dijon mustard
2 tablespoons sherry
1 1/2 cups heavy cream
2 egg yolks
1/4 cup grated Parmesan
   cheese
Lemon wedges and sliced
   black olives
Salt, black pepper, and
   cayenne, to taste

1. Boil the lobsters for 10 minutes or until slightly undercooked. Remove the claws from the body. Cut the lobsters in half lengthwise and loosen—but do not remove—the tail meat. Remove meat from claws and knuckles. Set aside.

2. Melt the butter in a skillet. Add the green pepper, pimentos, and mushrooms, and sauté over medium heat until vegetables are quite tender, about 5 minutes.

3. Stir in the mustard and sherry. Add the cream and bring to a boil. Reduce heat and simmer about 5 minutes, until the mixture begins to thicken.

4. Place the lobster, cut side down, over the cream mixture and simmer 2–3 minutes to heat the lobster through. Remove the lobster to a serving plate, cut side up, and cover to keep warm. Keep the cream mixture over the heat but reduce the heat to very low.

5. In a small bowl, whisk together egg yolks with a small amount of the hot cream mixture. Add the yolk mixture and the Parmesan back to remaining cream mixture and cook, stirring constantly, over low heat until mixture just coats the back of a spoon.

6. Remove the mixture from the heat, season with salt, black pepper, and cayenne. Add the claw and knuckle meat, tossing to coat. Arrange the claw and knuckle meat over the lobster. Garnish with olives and serve with lemon wedges.

Serves 2 as a main course

Lobster à la Newburg

Lobster Newburg is an American classic, having been around for at least a hundred years. It was originally called Lobster Wenburg. Legend has it that one Mr. Wenburg was a customer at Delmonico's restaurant in New York and came up with this lovely, rich dish. In time, however, Mr. Wenburg had a falling out with the management at Delmonico's and they changed the name to Newburg. Whatever the dish's origins, it is delicious.

1 tablespoon butter
8 ounces cooked lobster meat, cut into bite-sized chunks
2 tablespoons sherry
1 egg yolk
2 tablespoons cornstarch
2 cups milk

1. Melt the butter in a skillet and add the lobster. Cook for about 5 minutes, until lobster meat is warmed through. Whisk in the sherry.

2. In a small bowl, whisk together the yolk, cornstarch, and milk. Add this to the lobster and bring to a boil, stirring constantly. Reduce to a simmer and cook until mixture thickens, 2–3 minutes.

3. Serve over hot toast points or rice.

Serves 2

Lobster Ravioli

Lobster raviolis are often available in the fresh pasta section of your grocery store. Try this with a Caesar salad and some good Italian bread.

16 lobster-filled raviolis
1 tablespoon butter
1 teaspoon minced garlic
1/4 cup medium-dry
  sherry
1 cup heavy cream
Salt and white pepper, to taste
1/4 cup Romano cheese
1 teaspoon shredded basil
1 tablespoon minced chives
1 pound cooked lobster meat

1. In a large pot of salted water, cook raviolis according to package instructions. Drain and set aside.

2. In a skillet, heat butter with garlic until garlic begins to sizzle.

3. Add sherry to deglaze. Add cream, bring to a boil, then simmer until mixture reduces by about half. Add lobster meat and heat until just warmed through.

4. Season to taste with salt and pepper. Add cooked raviolis and toss gently to coat.

5. Transfer to a serving platter or to individual serving plates, sprinkle with Romano cheese, and garnish with chives and basil.

Serves 4

Sautéed Lobster Scampi

In this country, scampi refers to a method of preparation using olive oil, or butter and garlic. In Europe, it refers to a particular type of shrimp, although they are often prepared as they are in this recipe. Confusing, but delicious.

4 lobsters, 1 1/4 pounds each, or 1 pound of lobster meat
6 tablespoons butter, divided
1 tablespoon minced garlic
1 tablespoon minced fresh basil
1 teaspoon minced fresh chives
2 cups Roma tomatoes, canned or fresh, chopped
1/4 cup white wine
1 pound linguine (or your favorite pasta), cooked according to package directions
2 tablespoons Italian parsley, chopped

1. Boil lobsters for 10 minutes or until slightly undercooked. Remove the meat from the shell. Cut meat into large chunks. Set aside.

2. In a large sauté pan, melt 4 tablespoons of the butter. Add the garlic and sauté until garlic softens.

3. Add basil, chives, tomatoes, and white wine, and sauté for 3–4 minutes. Swirl in the remaining 2 tablespoons of butter.

4. When the butter is completely incorporated, add the lobster and cook until the lobster is warmed through. Serve over linguine. Garnish with parsley before serving.

Serves 4

New England Seafood Pie

This is true New England comfort food. At the Union Oyster House, the dish is topped with a potato crust. But a pie crust or a biscuit topping would also be delicious. You can use any combination of fish and shellfish, so experiment with your favorites.

1 cup chopped carrots
1 cup chopped onion
1 cup chopped leeks
1 tablespoon melted butter
1 pound firm white fish,
   cut into 1-inch chunks
1/2 pound sea scallops
1/2 pound shrimp
1/2 pint freshly shucked
   oysters
1 tablespoon minced fresh sage
1 tablespoon minced fresh
   thyme
1/2 cup white wine
2 tablespoons cornstarch
1/4 cup fish stock
Salt and pepper, to taste
Mashed potatoes, for topping

1. Preheat oven to 425°F. In a large pot, sauté vegetables in butter for 3–4 minutes, or until they begin to soften.

2. Add the seafood and sauté 2–3 minutes.

3. Add the herbs and wine, and simmer for 2 minutes.

4. In a small bowl, whisk together cornstarch and fish stock. Whisk the cornstarch mixture into the seafood mixture and simmer for 3–4 minutes, or until it thickens.

5. Spoon the mixture into a large casserole dish and allow to cool slightly, about 15 minutes. Season to taste with salt and pepper.

6. Cover the casserole with mashed potatoes (or other desired crust) and bake 25–30 minutes, until golden brown and bubbling.

Serves 4-6

Sautéed Seafood Medley

This flavorful Mediterranean-inspired dish includes calamari, small tender squid that cook very quickly. As with any seafood, but particularly calamari, it's important not to overcook them as they become rubbery.

1 tablespoon olive oil
2 teaspoons minced garlic
1/2 teaspoon crushed red
  pepper flakes
8 cherrystone clams
8 mussels
2 tablespoons white wine
1/4 cup clam juice
1/2 pound firm white fish
  fillets, cut into large chunks
1/4 pound calamari, sliced
  into rings
1 cup prepared marinara sauce

1. In a large, heavy-bottomed skillet, heat oil over high heat. Add garlic and red pepper, and sauté for a few seconds, until garlic softens.

2. Add clams, mussels, white wine, and clam juice. Simmer, covered, for about 5 minutes, or until clams and mussels open.

3. Add white fish and calamari, and cook for 1–2 minutes.

4. Add marinara sauce and cook for 2–3 minutes, or until white fish and calamari are cooked through. Serve over pasta, polenta, or rice.

Serves 2

Seafood Primavera

Although Italians have always used the most seasonal produce in their cooking, this dish was reputedly invented on this side of the Atlantic by the Italian-American owner of New York's famed Le Cirque. *Primavera* is the Italian word for spring, and this dish includes a variety of fresh vegetables along with fresh New England seafood.

4 tablespoons olive oil
2 cloves garlic, minced
1/2 cup thinly sliced carrots
3/4 cup broccoli florets
3/4 cup zucchini, cut in half
   lengthwise, then sliced
3/4 cup green peas
3/4 cup sliced mushrooms
6 medium shrimp, peeled
6 sea scallops, halved if
   extra large
4 ounces cooked lobster meat
1/4 cup white wine
1 cup Fish Velouté
   (see page 74)
1/3 cup tomato sauce
1/2 pound linguine, cooked
   and hot
Salt and pepper, to taste
Finely chopped parsley,
   for garnish

1. In a skillet, heat the oil and garlic until the garlic begins to sizzle. Add the carrots and broccoli, and sauté for 2–3 minutes.

2. Add the zucchini, peas, and mushrooms, and sauté for 2–3 minutes, or until vegetables are just barely cooked through.

3. Add the shrimp, scallops, lobster, and white wine. Simmer over low heat for 2–3 minutes, or until shrimp and scallops are cooked through and lobster is heated through.

4. Add velouté and tomato sauce, and simmer for 1–2 minutes.

5. Serve over the linguine. Season with salt and pepper, and garnish with chopped parsley.

Serves 2-4

Seafood Jambalaya

Jambalaya is a wonderful Cajun dish from Louisiana. There are many varieties—some without any seafood at all. But the Andouille sausage is great, whether paired with seafood, chicken, or alligator! If you can't find Andouille, substitute smoked sausage. The tomato and sausage mixture is even better when made a day ahead. You can cook the seafood and add it in right before serving.

3 tablespoons vegetable oil, divided
1 cup diced ham
1 cup diced Andouille sausage
1 tablespoon minced garlic
1 cup chopped onion
1 cup chopped green pepper
1 cup diced celery
1–2 minced jalapeños
6-ounce can of tomato paste
2 28-ounce cans crushed tomatoes
1/2 teaspoon cayenne pepper, or to taste
1 teaspoon cumin
1 tablespoon gumbo filé powder
Salt, to taste
1 pound sea scallops
1 pound large shrimp
1 quart mussels
1 cup fish stock or white wine
3–4 cups of cooked rice

1. In a stockpot, heat 1 tablespoon of oil. Add ham and Andouille, and cook over medium-high heat, about 5 minutes, allowing the meat to brown a little.

2. Add another tablespoon of the oil, garlic, onion, green pepper, celery, and jalapeños to the pan. Sauté until soft. Add tomato paste and stir well.

3. Add tomatoes, cayenne pepper, cumin, filé powder, and salt. Stir well and simmer for 20 minutes.

4. In a sauté pan, heat remaining table-spoon of oil. Add scallops and sear for 2–3 minutes. Stir in shrimp and sauté until they begin to turn pink. Add mussels and fish stock or wine, and cover. Simmer just until mussels open.

5. Stir rice and seafood into the tomato mixture, garnishing the top with some of the mussels.

Serves 6–8

Soft-Shell Crabs

Soft-shell crabs are blue crabs that are harvested between the times when they shed their shell (in order to grow) and the new shell has hardened. Although frozen soft-shell crabs are available year-round, the season for fresh is generally late spring. It's a strange thing to eat the whole crab, but they are incredibly delicious and quite simple to prepare. Ask your fishmonger to "dress" them for you if possible. Otherwise a quick Internet search for "blue crabs" yields a host of sites with instructions, recipes, and background.

1 stick of butter
8 soft-shell crabs, dressed
Juice of 1 lemon
1/4 cup fish stock (see page 72)
1 tablespoon chopped parsley
Lemon wedges, for serving

1. Melt butter in a large skillet until hot but not browned. Add crabs to pan, top shell down. Sauté for 2 minutes, or until golden brown. Turn crabs and cook for 2–3 minutes, or until cooked through.

2. Remove crabs from pan and keep warm.

3. Deglaze pan with lemon juice. Stir in fish stock.

4. Serve two crabs per person and pour pan juices over the crabs. Garnish with parsley and serve with lemon wedges.

Serves 4

Crab Cakes

Crab cakes are great with tartar or cocktail sauce, or just some fresh-squeezed lemon.

1 pound Jonah crab leg meat
1 tablespoon mayonnaise
1 egg
1 teaspoon chopped parsley
1 tablespoon minced red bell
  pepper
1/2 teaspoon Old Bay
  Seasoning
1/2 teaspoon mustard powder
5 dashes Worcestershire sauce
2 cups Panko (Japanese)
  bread crumbs
Salt and pepper, to taste
Olive oil or butter, for frying

1. Preheat oven to 400°F. Gently mix together all ingredients except oil or butter. Divide into eight cakes.

2. Heat butter or oil in a skillet and sauté crab cakes on both sides until golden brown.

3. Transfer to a baking sheet and bake for 5–10 minutes, until just cooked through.

Makes 8 cakes

Yankee Fish Cakes

When fresh fish wasn't available, this dish likely would have been made with salt cod, which is still widely available in the seafood department of the grocery store. If you're feeling adventurous, try the recipes with salt cod. Just be sure to rinse and soak it according to the package directions to get rid of the excess salt.

1 cup finely diced celery
1 cup finely diced onion
1 cup finely diced or grated carrot
4 tablespoons butter
1 1/2 pounds boneless white fish, such as cod, haddock, or hake, cut into 2-inch chunks
1/4 cup fish stock
2 cups mashed potatoes
2 teaspoons Old Bay Seasoning
1 teaspoon dried thyme
1 teaspoon Worcestershire sauce
2 eggs, whisked
1 cup Panko (Japanese) bread crumbs
Oil or butter, for sautéing
Salt and white pepper, to taste
Tartar sauce, for serving

1. Preheat oven to 400 In a large skillet, sauté vegetables in butter for 3–5 minutes until soft. Add fish and fish stock and cook, covered, for 5–7 minutes, or until fish begins to flake apart.

2. Remove from heat and mash the fish apart into flakes. Stir in mashed potatoes and seasonings. Allow mixture to cool to room temperature.

3. Gently mix in eggs and bread crumbs. Season to taste with salt and white pepper. Divide into cakes.

4. Heat oil or butter in a skillet and sauté fish cakes over medium-high heat until golden brown, turning once, about 2–3 minutes on each side. Place cakes in the oven and cook for another 6–8 minutes or until heated through. Serve hot with tartar sauce.

Makes 10-12 cakes

Baked Stuffed Haddock

Haddock is one of New Englanders' favorite fishes and is found on menus from the humblest fried-fish shacks to top-notch restaurants. But in the eighteenth and nineteenth centuries, haddock was considered a poor relation of cod—primarily because it didn't take to salting as well. In the latter half of the nineteenth century, as fresh fish grew more popular than salted, haddock began to be fully appreciated.

2 1/2 tablespoons butter, divided
1/4 cup chopped celery
1/4 cup chopped onion
1/2 cup tomato purée
1/4 teaspoon sugar
1 tablespoon flour
2 cups crushed saltines or buttery crackers
1 tablespoon finely minced celery
Salt and pepper, to taste
6 haddock fillets, 5–6 ounces each

1. Preheat oven to 400°F. Heat 1/2 tablespoon of the butter in a skillet, and sauté celery and onion for 2–3 minutes, until soft.

2. Add tomato purée and sugar. Simmer for 10 minutes.

3. Add flour and cook, stirring constantly, until thickened, about 2–3 minutes. Keep warm over low heat.

4. Melt the remaining 2 tablespoons butter in a second skillet. Remove from heat, and stir in crackers and minced celery. Season to taste with salt and pepper.

5. Lay haddock fillets over a lightly greased baking dish. Spread about 1/2 cup cracker stuffing over each fillet and bake for 10–12 minutes, or until haddock is just cooked through.

6. Transfer to a serving platter or to individual plates, and spoon tomato sauce alongside.

Serves 6

Shrimp Scampi

The name of this dish would likely confuse many Europeans as *scampi* is the Italian name for a type of shrimp or prawn. In this country, the word *scampi* usually refers to a method of preparing seafood with butter, olive oil, and lots of garlic.

4 tablespoons butter

4 tablespoons olive oil

2 tablespoons minced garlic

1 1/2 pounds large shrimp, peeled and deveined

3 tablespoons chopped fresh Italian or flat-leaf parsley, divided

2 tablespoons chopped fresh basil

1 tablespoon lemon juice

Salt and pepper, to taste

1 pound linguine or spaghetti

1. In a large pot, bring water for pasta to a boil.

2. In a skillet over medium-high heat, melt the butter with the olive oil until butter begins to sizzle. Add the garlic and cook for 1–2 minutes. Add the shrimp and cook for about 2 minutes.

3. Turn the shrimp over, add 2 tablespoons of the parsley, the basil, lemon juice, salt, and pepper, and cook for 2–3 minutes longer, until shrimp are just cooked through. Keep warm.

4. Cook pasta until al dente. Drain, reserving 1/3 cup pasta water. Add pasta and reserved liquid to shrimp mixture and toss well. Garnish with remaining parsley and serve immediately.

Serves 4-6

Blackened Shrimp with Roasted Red Pepper Sauce

Blackening is a classic Cajun method of cooking seafood, made famous by New Orleans chef Paul Prudhomme. Use the largest shrimp your budget will allow, as these stand up to this high-heat, intensely flavored recipe.

5 teaspoons paprika

1 teaspoon ground dried oregano

1 teaspoon ground dried thyme

1 teaspoon cayenne pepper (add more or use less, to taste)

1 teaspoon garlic salt

1/2 teaspoon white pepper

1/2 teaspoon black pepper

16 large shrimp, peeled and deveined

1 cup melted butter

Roasted Red Pepper Sauce (see page 79)

1. Preheat a skillet—preferably cast iron—until very hot. This may take 5 minutes or so. You want the pan to be almost red hot.

2. Combine all the dry ingredients in a plate or shallow bowl.

3. Dip the shrimp in the melted butter, then coat them completely with spice mixture. Place the shrimp in the hot skillet (in batches if necessary, so as not to crowd them) and cook 2 minutes. Be careful—this will smoke a lot.

4. Flip the shrimp over and cook the other side. Drizzle the remaining butter on the cooked side.

5. Cook for 2–3 minutes, until just cooked through. Serve immediately with Roasted Red Pepper Sauce.

Serves 4

Baked Scrod

There are many theories about the origin of the word scrod. One theory is that it is a derivation of the Dutch for "piece cut off," another that a Boston fish market or restaurant listed "Special Catch Recorded on Day." We'll never know the true origins, but the species is generally regarded as a young member of the cod family, usually two pounds or less.

1/2 cup unseasoned bread crumbs

1/2 cup finely crushed potato chips

1/2 cup finely crushed snack crackers

1/2 teaspoon dried thyme

1/2 teaspoon minced garlic

2 tablespoons melted butter

4 white fish fillets, 6–8 ounces each, such as cod, haddock, or cusk

1/2 cup white wine

Salt and pepper, to taste

4 pats (1/2 tablespoon) butter

1. Preheat oven to 400°F. In a large bowl, mix together bread crumbs, potato chips, snack crackers, thyme, garlic, salt, and pepper. Add the melted butter and mix well.

2. Lightly grease a baking sheet. Dip the fish fillets in the white wine, then season to taste with salt and pepper.

3. Dredge fillets in crumb mixture to coat. Arrange fillets on the baking sheet and place a pat of the chilled butter over each fillet.

4. Bake at 375°F for 10–12 minutes, until just cooked through but still moist.

Serves 4

Poached Halibut

Halibut is a large North Atlantic flatfish much prized for its flavor and texture. Halibut can grow as large as seven hundred pounds and up to nine feet long, but most of the Atlantic halibut caught these days are in the fifty- to one-hundred-pound range. This is a great, simple preparation that lets the flavor of the fish shine through.

3 tablespoons olive oil
1 cup diced red onion
4 cloves garlic, sliced thin
2 cups diced tomatoes
1/2 cup dry white wine
4 halibut fillets, 7–8 ounces each
2 teaspoons minced fresh thyme
Salt and pepper, to taste

1. Heat oil in a large skillet over medium-high heat. Add the onion and garlic, and sauté until tender, about 3–4 minutes.

2. Add the tomatoes and white wine, bring to a boil, then simmer about five minutes.

3. Add the halibut fillets and season with thyme, salt, and pepper. Cover and simmer for 10–12 minutes, or until just cooked through and beginning to flake. Serve fillets over rice or pasta with the pan juices drizzled on top.

Serves 4

Poached Sole with Cucumber Dill Sauce

Sole is a delicate, white fish that goes well with mild sauces and also lends itself well to a quick sauté in a fry pan with butter and lemon. You could also use flounder or tilapia, or other delicate white fish fillets as well as salmon.

1 cup sour cream
1/4 cup mayonnaise
1 tablespoon dried dillweed
1 cup diced cucumber, seeded
  and peeled
1 teaspoon lemon juice
Salt and pepper, to taste
1 1/2 pounds sole fillets
2 tablespoons dry white wine
1 cup fish stock (see page 72)

1. Preheat oven to 350°F. Combine the first six ingredients in a small bowl and mix well. Refrigerate until ready to serve.

2. Lightly grease a baking dish. Arrange the sole fillets over the bottom and season with salt and pepper. Drizzle the fish with white wine and fish stock, and bake for 10–12 minutes, or until just cooked through. Serve with the cucumber dill sauce.

Serves 4

Littlenecks and Linguine with Shitake Mushrooms

Boston's North End is known for its wonderful Italian groceries and restaurants. This is a Union Oyster House variation on the classic Italian linguine with red clam sauce.

4 tablespoons olive oil

2 cups thickly sliced shitake mushrooms

2 tablespoons minced garlic

1 teaspoon red pepper flakes

3 dozen littleneck clams, cleaned

2 cups white wine

1 cup chopped plum tomatoes

3 cups clam juice

1 cup minced parsley, divided

1 pound linguine

1. In a large skillet, heat olive oil over medium-high heat. Add the mushrooms, garlic, and red pepper flakes, and cook until the mushrooms are beginning to brown.

2. Add the littlenecks and wine. Cover and simmer until the littlenecks begin to open. Remove the opened littlenecks from the pan and set aside.

3. When all of the littlenecks have been removed, add to the skillet plum tomatoes, clam juice, and 1/2 cup parsley. Simmer over medium-high heat for 30 minutes, or until the mixture has reduced by about half. There should be about 2 1/2 cups liquid.

4. Cook linguine according to package instructions.

5. Add the reserved clams to tomato sauce and cook for 1–2 minutes, until the clams are reheated. Serve over linguine and garnish with the remaining parsley.

Serves 4

Grilled Swordfish and Vegetables with Lemon Butter

There is nothing like swordfish on the grill, but be sure not to overcook the steaks as they tend to dry out.

1/2 cup butter

Juice and zest of 1 lemon

1 clove garlic, minced

1 teaspoon minced fresh thyme

4 swordfish steaks, about 8 ounces each, cut about 3/4-inch thick

Salt and pepper to taste

12 baby carrots, peeled and blanched

2 red peppers, quartered lengthwise, seeds removed

2 green peppers, quartered lengthwise, seeds removed

2 medium zucchini, sliced 1/2-inch thick on the bias

1 pound asparagus, trimmed and blanched

1. Preheat the grill to medium-high. In a small saucepan, melt the butter with the lemon juice, lemon zest, and thyme.

2. Season the swordfish steaks on both sides with salt and pepper. Set aside.

3. Brush the vegetables generously with the butter mixture. Season with garlic, salt and pepper, and grill for 5–10 minutes, until just cooked through, turning as needed. When the vegetables are done, remove to a baking pan or an ovenproof platter, and set on the upper shelf of the grill or in a low oven to keep warm.

4. Brush the swordfish steaks on both sides with the lemon butter and grill in the center of the grill, about 5–10 minutes per side or until just cooked through. Brush the steaks with additional lemon butter and serve immediately with the roasted vegetables.

Serves 4

Side Dishes

The Union Oyster House focuses on simple, traditional New England accompaniments to the restaurant's dishes. Classics such as Boston Baked Beans and Cornbread date back to the earliest days of the Massachusetts Bay Colony and, more than likely, may even be variations on dishes the Native Americans were cooking when the first settlers arrived.

Boston Baked Beans

Boston's nickname is "Beantown" due to the popularity of this age-old dish. Although most Europeans would have had their own bean recipes from their native lands—for example, cassoulet from France, pease porridge from England and pasta fagiole from Italy—the colonists were likely to have been inspired by the way the Native Americans prepared their beans with bear fat and maple syrup in an earthenware pot that was set in the ground and covered with ash. This recipe was adapted and came to include bacon or salt pork and molasses.

1 pound dried white pea
  or Navy beans
3 ounces diced salt pork
1 cup diced onion
2 cups tomato juice
1 cup molasses
1 tablespoon brown sugar
1 tablespoon mustard
1 tablespoon garlic powder

1. Cover beans with 2 quarts cold water and soak 12 hours or overnight. Drain.

2. Preheat oven to 325°F. In a large stockpot, cook salt pork over medium heat until rendered.

3. Add the onion and cook until tender. Add tomato juice, molasses, sugar, mustard, and garlic powder. Mix well. Add beans and enough water so that the beans are covered by about 1 inch of liquid.

4. Bring to a boil, then remove from heat and place in the oven, covered. Bake for 2 hours, stirring occasionally, or until beans are soft and sauce has thickened. Add more liquid if beans begin to dry out. If you'd like a slightly crusty top, remove the cover for the last half hour.

Serves 8

The Boston Molasses Flood

Boston was the distilling capital of the colonies. Hence, it had ample supplies of molasses that came north from the cane plantations. Rum was distilled and shipped across the Atlantic along with other goods to purchase slaves, who were then sent to the cane plantations of the Caribbean, where the cycle began again. This pattern became known as the Triangular Trade, and it existed in some form until the 1830s when the British parliament abolished slavery in its territories.

Nonetheless, Boston was still awash in molasses well into the twentieth century, quite literally on January 15, 1919. Patrons at the oyster bar would likely have heard the explosion of a molasses tank a few blocks away on Commercial Street. The tank caused nearly a dozen deaths and more than fifty injuries when it exploded, and released some two million gallons of molasses into the streets. A *New York Times* reporter described the scene this way: "Wagons, carts and motor trucks were overturned. A number of horses were killed. The street was strewn with debris intermixed with molasses and all traffic was stopped." Some Bostonians claim you can still detect the smell of molasses downtown on a hot day!

Old-Fashioned Codfish Mashed Potatoes

In the early days, it's likely that this dish often would have been made using salt cod—a staple of the New England diet from the days of the earliest settlers. You can still purchase salt cod in the preserved fish sections of many supermarkets. If you'd like to try preparing the fish the old-fashioned way, just follow the package directions for soaking and reconstituting the cod and go easy on any additional salt.

3 cups peeled potatoes cut into 1-inch dice

6 tablespoons butter, divided

12 ounces boneless, skinless cod fillets

2 teaspoons minced garlic

1/2 cup milk

1/2 cup half-and-half

Salt and pepper, to taste

1 tablespoon chopped parsley

1. In a stockpot, boil potatoes until soft.

2. While potatoes are simmering, melt 2 tablespoons of the butter in a skillet until butter begins to brown. Add cod fillets and cook for 2–3 minutes, until they begin to brown slightly.

3. Add garlic, turn fish over and cook for another 2–3 minutes on the other side, until lightly browned.

4. Add milk, cover, and bring to a boil. Reduce heat and simmer about 5 minutes, or until fish begins to flake apart. Remove from heat and keep warm.

5. Drain the potatoes and transfer to a bowl. Add the remaining 4 tablespoons butter, half-and-half, salt, and pepper. Mash with a potato masher until smooth.

6. Gently fold in cooked cod. Season to taste and garnish with parsley.

Serves 6

Cornbread

Cornbread is believed to be one of the original American dishes. It's likely that Native Americans had been making similar dishes long before the first settlers arrived. There are variations from region to region, and cornbread also is frequently called Johnny Cake. As early as 1787, the author of *The Compleat American Housewife* says, "Our citizens both high and low, mean and genteel, love Johnny Cake." The Union Oyster House is justly famous for its recipe.

3/4 cup butter, softened
2 cups sugar
2 tablespoons baking powder
2 teaspoons salt
3 eggs
1/2 cup vegetable oil
1 cup cornmeal
3 1/4 cups flour
2 cups milk

1. Preheat oven to 350°F. In a mixing bowl, cream together butter, sugar, baking powder, and salt.

2. Add eggs, one at a time, beating well after each addition.

3. Add vegetable oil and cornmeal, and mix for about 30 seconds. Scrape sides of bowl and beat about 15 seconds more.

4. Add flour and mix. Add milk and beat until smooth. Scrape sides and mix for a few seconds longer.

5. Grease and flour a 13 x 9inch baking pan. Pour batter into pan and bake for 30–35 minutes, or until a toothpick inserted in the center comes out clean.

Serves 6-8

Old-Fashioned Oyster Stuffing

We think of oyster stuffing as a Thanksgiving dish traditionally served with turkey. But in the *Boston Cooking School Cook Book* by Fannie Farmer, there are two recipes for fish with oyster stuffing. Oysters were so popular in the 1800s, they made their way into all kinds of dishes and menus.

2 loaves sliced white bread, diced into 1/2-inch cubes
1/2 cup butter
3 cups diced celery
3 cups diced onion
1 teaspoon dried thyme
1 teaspoon dried sage
2 cups freshly shucked oysters, with their juices
3–4 eggs, beaten
Salt and pepper, to taste

1. Preheat oven to 200°F. Place bread on a baking sheet and bake for about 1 hour, until dried. Remove from oven and place in a large bowl.

2. In a large skillet, melt butter over medium heat until it begins to foam. Add celery and onion and cook until vegetables are tender, about 5 minutes.

3. Add herbs, oysters, and their juices and cook for about 2 minutes, until oysters begin to plump and their edges curl.

4. Pour the oyster mixture over the bread and toss well to combine.

5. Add eggs and season to taste with salt and pepper.

Makes enough to stuff a 15- to 18-pound turkey

Hearty Wild Rice

Wild rice and maize are two of the few cereal crops native to America. Both were successfully cultivated by Native Americans long before the first settlers arrived. This blend of white and wild rice makes a great hearty side dish.

2 tablespoons butter
1/2 cup diced carrot
1/2 cup diced celery
1/2 cup diced onion
1/2 cup long-grain wild rice
1/2 cup white rice
2 cups chicken stock
1 teaspoon dried thyme
1 teaspoon dried sage
1/2 teaspoon white pepper
Salt, to taste

1. In a saucepan over medium-high heat, melt butter until it begins to foam. Add vegetables and cook until they just begin to soften, about 5 minutes.

2. Add wild rice and white rice, and stir to coat.

3. Add chicken stock, herbs, pepper, and salt, and bring to a boil. Reduce heat and simmer, covered, for 20 minutes or until rice is cooked through. Fluff with a fork before serving.

Serves 4

Rice Pilaf

Cooking rice in chicken stock and adding onion and herbs gives an otherwise plain side dish extra zip. This is great alongside any grilled or poached fish.

6 tablespoons butter, divided

1/2 cup finely diced onion

1 cup white rice

2 cups chicken stock

1 bay leaf

1 tablespoon minced fresh parsley

1 teaspoon minced fresh thyme

Salt and pepper, to taste

1. Preheat oven to 350°F. Heat 2 tablespoons of butter over medium heat in an ovenproof skillet. Add the onion and sauté until translucent, about 3–4 minutes. Add the rice and cook, stirring occasionally, for 2–3 minutes more.

2. Add the chicken stock, bay leaf, parsley, thyme, salt, and pepper, and bring to a boil. Cover the pan with a tight-fitting lid and simmer for 20 minutes or until rice is tender. Remove from heat and stir in the remaining butter.

Serves 4–6

Spinach with Lemon and Walnuts

This light but flavorful side dish is perfect with just about any seafood entrée. Before it is cooked, it may seem like a lot of spinach, but it wilts down quickly. Try not to overcook to preserve the color and texture of the fresh spinach.

1 tablespoon olive oil
1/4 cup chopped walnuts
2 cloves garlic, minced
2 tablespoons fresh lemon
  juice
1 pound fresh spinach, washed,
  stems removed
Salt and pepper, to taste

1. In a skillet, heat the olive oil over medium-high heat. Sauté walnuts until slightly browned.

2. Add the garlic and lemon juice, and sauté for 1 minute. Add the spinach, salt and pepper and cook until the spinach is just wilted. Serve immediately.

Serves 4

Roasted Shallots

This method of cooking brings out the natural sweetness of the shallots. This would make a good side dish for grilled fish, roasted chicken, or beef.

1 pound peeled shallots
3 tablespoons balsamic
  vinegar, divided
2 tablespoons olive oil
1 tablespoon minced fresh
  thyme
Salt and pepper, to taste

1. Preheat oven to 400°F. In a bowl, toss the shallots with 2 tablespoons of the balsamic vinegar, olive oil, thyme, salt, and pepper.

2. Spread onto a baking sheet and bake for 30–35 minutes, until shallots are tender but not falling apart. Drizzle with the remaining tablespoon of balsamic vinegar.

Serves 4–6

Desserts

The desserts at the Union Oyster House are classic New England fare—almost a time capsule in themselves. From Indian Pudding to New York Cheesecake, they are simple and delicious, and incorporate great local ingredients.

Apple Pie

Why the phrase as "American as apple pie" was coined (the entire epigram is actually "as American as baseball and apple pie") is a mystery; Europeans had been making apple pies, tarts, and strudels for quite some time. Baseball, sure, but apple pie? Still, the phrase stuck. And during World War II, when you asked a soldier why he was going to war, a stock answer was "For mom and apple pie."

1 cup water
1/2 cup butter, softened
2 tablespoons lemon juice
1/2 tablespoon cinnamon
1 teaspoon ground cloves
2 tablespoons cornstarch
1/3 cup sugar
6-8 Cortland or McIntosh
  apples, peeled, cored,
  and sliced
Pie Crust (recipe follows,
  or use you favorite prepared
  crust)
1 egg, beaten

1. Preheat oven to 350°F. In a small saucepan, whisk together all ingredients except apples, pie crust, and egg. Bring to a boil, whisking constantly.

2. Pour the cornstarch mixture over the apples in a large bowl and toss well to combine. Allow to cool.

3. Line a 9-inch pie pan with one of the pie crusts. Place prepared apple filling in the crust. Brush edges with egg. Cover pie with remaining crust. Brush top with egg and place four or five slits in the top. Bake for 45–50 minutes, until golden brown and bubbling.

Makes a 9-inch pie

Pie Crust

2 1/2 cups flour
1/4 teaspoon salt
1/2 cup cold butter, diced
1/2 cup shortening
1/2 cup cold milk

1. Sift together flour and salt.

2. Cut butter and shortening into flour until it resembles coarse meal.

3. Add milk and knead gently, just to form a dough. Dough will be soft. Chill at least 1 hour, or overnight, before using.

Makes two 8- or 9-inch crusts

Fruitful Shores

When the first settlers arrived, they found an abundance of native fruits: cranberries, blueberries, blackberries, raspberries, currants, grapes, cherries, and plums, among others. In what is now Portsmouth, New Hampshire, the new arrivals found so many fields of plump native strawberries that they named their first settlement "Strawbery Banke." Not surprisingly, Native Americans had, for many years, been making good use of all the natural resources available, and used various fruits to create dyes, medicines, and juices. The fruits were dried and preserved for the off season.

Oddly, apples—which we think of as quintessentially American—were first planted by early European settlers. The trees thrived and grew better in North American soil than in European soil, most settlers agreed. The first apple orchard in the Massachusetts Bay Colony was planted in 1625 on what is now Boston's Beacon Hill.

Apple Crisp

This dish is best served warm with ice cream. Try a vanilla caramel flavor for an extra treat. At the holidays, the Union Oyster House adds cranberries to this dish.

For the Crisp Topping
1 3/4 cups rolled oats or plain oatmeal
1 cup flour
3/4 cup brown sugar, packed
3/4 cup butter, softened
1 cup chopped walnuts

For the Apple Crisp
3 large Cortland apples, peeled, cored, and thickly sliced
3 large Granny Smith apples, peeled, cored, and thickly sliced
3/4 cup frozen cranberries
1/2 tablespoon cinnamon
3/4 cup sugar

1. Preheat oven to 350°F.

2. To make the Crisp Topping: Mix together oats, flour, walnuts, and brown sugar. Add butter and mix until crumbly.

3. To make the Apple Crisp: Toss together apples, cranberries, cinnamon, and sugar. Place filling in a deep baking dish.

4. Spread Crisp Topping evenly over top.

5. Bake for 40–50 minutes, until browned and bubbling.

Serves 6-8

New York Cheesecake

This recipe gives a nod to Boston's neighbor to the south. New Yorkers claim that theirs is the only "true" cheesecake, unadulterated by added ingredients or toppings.

1 1/2 pounds cream cheese
1 1/4 cups sugar, divided
3 eggs
1/2 teaspoon vanilla
1 tablespoon lemon juice
2 tablespoons butter

1. Preheat oven to 300°F. Cream together cream cheese and 1 cup of the sugar until smooth, about 5 minutes.

2. Add eggs and beat 2–3 minutes, scraping bowl occasionally.

3. Add vanilla and lemon juice, and blend thoroughly.

4. Coat a 10-inch springform pan with the butter. Sprinkle remaining 1/4 cup sugar over the surface of the pan to evenly coat.

5. Pour cheesecake mixture into the prepared pan and place in a roasting pan. Pour warm water into the roasting pan and bake for 3 hours. Shut off heat and leave cheesecake in oven for half an hour to cool. Remove from water bath and cool thoroughly in refrigerator.

Serves 8–12

Gingerbread

Although gingerbread was a familiar English food—it is mentioned by Shakespeare—it had clearly not diminished in popularity by the late 1800s. Fannie Farmer's classic *Boston Cooking School Cook Book* contains no fewer than eight recipes for gingerbread, including Hot Water Gingerbread, Soft Molasses Gingerbread, and Cambridge Gingerbread, which is similar to this recipe.

1/2 cup vegetable oil
1/2 cup sugar
1 egg, beaten
1 cup molasses
2 1/2 cups sifted flour
1 1/2 teaspoons baking soda
1/2 teaspoon salt
1 teaspoon ginger
1 teaspoon cinnamon
1/2 teaspoon ground cloves
1 cup hot water

1. Preheat oven to 350°F. Grease and flour a 9- x 9-inch cake pan. Cream together oil and sugar until light and fluffy.

2. Add egg and molasses and mix well.

3. Add dry ingredients and mix to combine.

4. Add hot water and mix until smooth.

5. Pour into prepared pan and bake 30 minutes, or until a toothpick inserted into the center comes out clean.

Serves 6–8

Indian Pudding

Maybe the saying should have been "as American as Indian Pudding." This is one of the oldest recipes to be passed down from the original settlers. As late as 1900, cornmeal was known as Indian meal, as it was the Native Americans who introduced the settlers to this versatile ingredient.

5 cups milk, divided
2/3 cup yellow cornmeal
3/4 cup molasses
1/2 cup brown sugar
3/4 teaspoon salt
3 tablespoons butter
1 1/2 teaspoons ginger
1 teaspoon cinnamon
1/2 cup raisins
3 eggs, beaten

1. Preheat oven to 325°F. Scald 4 cups of the milk by heating until a skin forms on the top.

2. Whisk cornmeal together with 1/2 cup milk and slowly add to the scalded milk. Cook over medium heat, stirring constantly, for 15 minutes until mixture begins to thicken. Remove from heat.

3. Add molasses, sugar, salt, butter, ginger, cinnamon, and raisins, stirring well until butter melts.

4. Allow to cool slightly and beat in eggs.

5. Pour into a deep casserole dish and bake for 1 hour.

6. Stir in remaining 1/2 cup milk and bake for another 1 1/4 hours. Let stand for half an hour and serve warm with ice cream or whipped cream.

Serves 6-8

Boston Cream Pie

A trip to Boston wouldn't be complete without a taste of Boston Cream Pie—which is actually much more like a cake. The Union Oyster House recipe has been adapted here to make a quick and easy version for home cooks. *See photo on page 122.*

1 package yellow cake mix, prepared according to package instructions
1 package vanilla pudding mix, prepared according to package instructions
1 cup Chocolate Glaze (recipe below)

1. Slice the yellow cake into a top and a bottom layer. Remove the top layer and set aside. Spread the vanilla pudding evenly over the bottom layer.

2. Place the top layer over the vanilla pudding.

3. Pour the Chocolate Glaze evenly over the top, allowing it to drizzle down the sides. Refrigerate 1 hour before serving.

Serves 6-8

Chocolate Glaze

2 tablespoons water
1 tablespoon butter
1 tablespoon light corn syrup
2 tablespoons cocoa powder
3/4 cup confectioners' sugar
1/2 teaspoon vanilla

1. In a small saucepan over high heat, bring the water, butter, and corn syrup to a boil.

2. Remove from the heat and stir in the cocoa powder. Whisk in the confectioners' sugar and vanilla until smooth.

Makes 1 cup

Index